Celebrating Veterans Day

Katie Peters

GRL Consultant Diane Craig,
Certified Literacy Specialist

Lerner Publications ◆ Minneapolis

Note from a GRL Consultant
This Pull Ahead leveled book has been carefully designed for beginning readers. A team of guided reading literacy experts has reviewed and leveled the book to ensure readers pull ahead and experience success.

Lerner Publications
An imprint of Lerner Publishing Group, Inc.
241 First Avenue North
Minneapolis, MN 55401 USA

For reading levels and more information, look up this title at www.lernerbooks.com.

Main body text set in Memphis Pro 24/39
Typeface provided by Linotype.

Photo Acknowledgments
The images in this book are used with the permission of: © Africa Studio/Shutterstock Images, p. 3; © LightField Studios/Shutterstock Images, pp. 4–5; © vectorfusionart/Shutterstock Images, pp. 6–7, 16 (right); © Svitlana Hulko/Shutterstock Images, pp. 8–9, 16 (left); © Jacob Lund/Shutterstock Images, pp. 10–11; © wavebreakmedia/Shutterstock Images, pp. 12–13, 16 (middle); © Evgeny Atamanenko/Shutterstock Images, pp. 14–15.

Front Cover: © Evgeny Atamanenko/Shutterstock Images

Library of Congress Cataloging-in-Publication Data

Names: Peters, Katie, author.
Title: Celebrating Veterans Day / written by Katie Peters.
Description: Minneapolis, MN : Lerner Publications , 2026. | Series: Pull ahead readers, nonfiction. Let's celebrate holidays | Includes index. | Audience: Ages 4–7 | Audience: Grades K–1 | Summary: "Many people have soldiers in their family, and on Veterans Day we thank them for their service. Vibrant photographs and leveled text help readers salute our veterans. Pairs with the story, Sofia's Veterans Day Project"—Provided by publisher.
Identifiers: LCCN 2024038502 (print) | LCCN 2024038503 (ebook) | ISBN 9798765668771 (library binding) | ISBN 9798765684467 (paperback) | ISBN 9798765678817 (epub)
Subjects: LCSH: Veterans' Day—Juvenile literature.
Classification: LCC D671 .P47 2026 (print) | LCC D671 (ebook) | DDC 394.264—dc23/eng/20241118

LC record available at https://lccn.loc.gov/2024038502
LC ebook record available at https://lccn.loc.gov/2024038503

Manufactured in the United States of America
1 – CG – 7/15/25

Table of Contents

Celebrating Veterans Day

My family served in the military.

My mom served in the military.

My dad served in the military.

My aunt served in the military.

My grandpa served in the military.

On Veterans Day, we thank them for their service.

Did You See It?

dad

grandpa

mom

Index